AF413814

AN INTRODUCTION TO MACHINE LEARNING FOR EVERYONE

C. FANCY

M. ANAND

N. KRISHNARAJ

H. KARTHIKEYAN

Contents

ONE

INTRODUCTION

Machine learning, a transformative branch of AI, empowers computers to learn from data, uncovering patterns and making intelligent decisions without explicit programming. By leveraging supervised learning (think spam filtering) and unsupervised learning (think grouping similar customers), machine learning algorithms fuel innovations across industries. From healthcare diagnoses to self-driving cars, these algorithms automate tasks, unearth valuable insights, and make predictions that are revolutionizing our world. As we delve deeper into this field, ethical considerations like fairness and transparency become paramount to ensure responsible AI development. By understanding the core concepts and staying current on advancements, you can play a role in shaping the exciting future of machine learning.

What is Machine Learning?

Machine Learning (ML) is a branch of artificial intelligence (AI) that empowers systems to learn from data and make predictions or decisions without explicit programming. It's like teaching a computer to learn from experience, much like a human does.

Key Concepts:

Data is the lifeblood of machine learning algorithms. It's the raw material that these algorithms use to learn patterns, make predictions, and generate insights.

Structured Data:

Structured data is organized in a well-defined format, making it easy for machines to understand and process. It's typically stored in databases or spreadsheets, with each column representing a specific attribute and each row representing a data point. Examples of structured data include:

- **Spreadsheets:** Data tables with rows and columns.
- **Relational Databases:** Tables with defined relationships between them.
- **CSV Files:** Comma-separated values files.

Unstructured Data:

Unstructured data doesn't have a predefined format, making it more challenging to process. It's often found in text, images, audio, and video files. Examples of unstructured data include:

- **Text Documents:** Articles, emails, social media posts.
- **Images:** Photos, scanned documents, medical images.
- **Audio:** Speech recordings, music files.
- **Video:** Videos, movies, surveillance footage.

Why the Distinction Matters:

The type of data you have significantly impacts the machine learning techniques you can use. Structured data is often used with traditional machine learning algorithms like linear regression, decision trees, and support vector machines. Unstructured data, on the other hand, requires more advanced techniques like natural language processing (NLP) for text, computer vision for images, and audio/video processing for other media.

The Importance of Data Quality:

Regardless of the data type, the quality of your data is crucial. Poor-quality data can lead to inaccurate models and misleading results. Key aspects of data quality include:

- **Completeness:** Missing values can hinder analysis.

- **Accuracy:** Data should be correct and free from errors.
- **Consistency:** Data should be formatted consistently.
- **Relevance:** Data should be relevant to the problem you're trying to solve.

Algorithms are the mathematical recipes that guide machine learning models in their learning process. They're the tools that enable computers to sift through vast amounts of data, identify patterns, and make intelligent decisions.

Here's a deeper dive into the role of algorithms in machine learning:

Types of Machine Learning Algorithms

Machine learning algorithms can be broadly categorized into three main types:

1. **Supervised Learning:**

   - **Regression:** Predicting a continuous numerical value.

     - Examples: Predicting house prices, stock prices, or temperature.

   - **Classification:** Predicting a categorical value.

     - Examples: Email spam detection, medical diagnosis, or image recognition.

2. **Unsupervised Learning:**

   - **Clustering:** Grouping similar data points together.

     - Examples: Customer segmentation, document clustering, or image compression.

- ○ **Dimensionality Reduction:** Reducing the number of features in a dataset.

  - ▪ Examples: Principal Component Analysis (PCA) and t-SNE.

3. **Reinforcement Learning:**

   - ○ Learning through trial and error, interacting with an environment to maximize rewards.

     - ▪ Examples: Game playing, robotics, and self-driving cars.

How Algorithms Work

1. **Data Preparation:**

   - ○ Cleaning and preprocessing data to remove noise and inconsistencies.
   - ○ Feature engineering: Creating new features or transforming existing ones to improve model performance.

2. **Model Training:**

   - ○ The algorithm learns patterns from the training data.
   - ○ It adjusts its parameters to minimize the error between its predictions and the actual values.

3. **Model Evaluation:**

   - ○ The trained model is tested on a separate validation dataset to assess its accuracy and generalizability.

4. **Model Deployment:**

○ The model is deployed to make predictions on new, unseen data.

Popular Algorithms

- **Linear Regression**: Models the relationship between a dependent variable and one or more independent variables.
- **Logistic Regression:**[1] Used for classification tasks, predicting the probability of an event occurring.
- **Decision Trees:** Creates a tree-like model of decisions and their possible consequences.
- **Random Forest:** An ensemble method that combines multiple decision trees to improve accuracy.
- **Support Vector Machines (SVM):** Finds the optimal hyperplane to separate data points into different classes.
- **Naive Bayes:** Based on Bayes' theorem, used for classification tasks, especially text classification.
- **K-Nearest Neighbors (KNN):** Classifies data points based on the majority class of their nearest neighbors.
- **Neural Networks:** Inspired by the human brain, capable of learning complex patterns.

By understanding these algorithms and their applications, you can effectively leverage machine learning to solve a wide range of real-world problems.

Training is the core process in machine learning where an algorithm learns from a dataset. It's akin to educating a child: you expose them to various examples and experiences, and they gradually learn to recognize patterns and make informed decisions.

Here's a more detailed breakdown of the training process:

1. **Data Preparation:**

○ **Cleaning:** Removing noise, inconsistencies, and missing values.

- **Preprocessing:** Transforming data into a suitable format for the algorithm (e.g., normalization, feature scaling).
- **Feature Engineering:** Creating new features or transforming existing ones to improve model performance.

2. **Model Selection:**

- Choosing the appropriate algorithm based on the problem type (classification, regression, clustering, etc.) and the nature of the data.

3. **Model Training:**

- **Feeding the Data:** The algorithm is fed with the prepared training data.
- **Learning Patterns:** The algorithm identifies patterns and relationships within the data.
- **Parameter Adjustment:** The algorithm adjusts its internal parameters to minimize the error between its predictions and the actual values.
- **Optimization:** Techniques like gradient descent are used to optimize the parameters iteratively.

4. **Model Evaluation:**

- **Validation Set:** A portion of the data is held back to evaluate the model's performance on unseen data.
- **Performance Metrics:** Metrics like accuracy, precision, recall, F1-score, and mean squared error are used to assess the model's accuracy.

5. **Model Refinement:**

- If the model's performance is not satisfactory, adjustments are made to the data, algorithm, or hyperparameters.

- This iterative process continues until the desired level of performance is achieved.

By effectively training a machine learning model, we can empower it to make accurate predictions and decisions on new, unseen data.

Once a machine learning model has been trained on a sufficient amount of data, it becomes capable of making predictions or decisions on new, unseen data. This is the ultimate goal of the training process.

Here's a breakdown of how this works:

1. **Input Data:**

   - New, unseen data is fed into the trained model.

1. **Feature Extraction:**

   - The model extracts relevant features from the input data, similar to how it did during training.

2. **Model Processing:**

   - The model applies its learned patterns and relationships to the input data.

3. **Prediction or Decision:**

   - The model generates a prediction or makes a decision based on its analysis.

Examples of Predictions and Decisions:

- **Image Classification:** Identifying objects or scenes in images.

- **Natural Language Processing**: Understanding and generating human language.
- **Recommendation Systems**: Suggesting products or content based on user preferences.
- **Fraud Detection**: Identifying fraudulent transactions.
- **Medical Diagnosis**: Assisting in diagnosing diseases.
- **Self-Driving Cars**: Making real-time driving decisions.

Key Considerations for Model Deployment:

- **Model Performance**: Ensuring the model's accuracy and reliability on real-world data.
- **Model Interpretability**: Understanding the reasons behind the model's predictions.
- **Model Maintenance**: Regularly updating the model with new data to maintain its performance.
- **Ethical Considerations**: Addressing biases and ensuring fairness in model decisions.

By effectively deploying trained machine learning models, we can automate tasks, gain valuable insights, and drive innovation across various industries.

Real-world Applications:

Recommendation Systems: Recommendation systems are powerful tools that leverage data and algorithms to provide personalized suggestions to users. These systems are ubiquitous in our digital lives, influencing everything from the movies we watch on Netflix to the products we buy on Amazon.

How Do Recommendation Systems Work?

There are primarily two main approaches to building recommendation systems:

1. **Content-Based Filtering:**

- ○ **Understanding the User**: This approach analyzes a user's past behavior, such as items they've rated or purchased.
- ○ **Identifying Similar Items**: It then identifies items that are similar to those the user has interacted with in the past.
- ○ **Making Recommendations**: The system recommends these similar items to the user, assuming they will also enjoy them.

2. **Collaborative Filtering:**

- ○ **Finding Similar Users**: This approach finds other users with similar preferences or behaviors.
- ○ **Recommending Based on Peers**: It then recommends items that these similar users have enjoyed.
- ○ **Hybrid Approaches**: Often, a combination of content-based and collaborative filtering is used to provide more accurate and diverse recommendations.

Key Techniques and Considerations:

- **Feature Engineering**: Creating meaningful features from raw data is crucial. This involves techniques like text mining, natural language processing, and image analysis.
- **Matrix Factorization**: This technique decomposes a large user-item matrix into smaller matrices, capturing latent factors that explain user preferences and item characteristics.
- **Deep Learning**: Neural networks, especially deep learning models, are increasingly used for recommendation systems. They can learn complex patterns from large datasets.
- **Cold Start Problem**: When a new user or item is introduced, there's limited data to make accurate recommendations. Techniques like knowledge-based recommendation or hybrid approaches can help mitigate this.
- **Sparsity**: Real-world datasets are often sparse, meaning most users have only rated a small fraction of items. Matrix factorization and deep learning techniques can handle sparsity

effectively.

- **Ethical Considerations:** Recommendation systems can influence user behavior, so it's important to consider fairness, diversity, and transparency in their design and implementation.

Image and Speech Recognition: Image and speech recognition have revolutionized the way we interact with technology. These technologies, powered by artificial intelligence, enable machines to understand and interpret visual and auditory information, opening up a world of possibilities.

Image Recognition

Image recognition, a subset of computer vision, involves the process of identifying and classifying objects within an image. It's a complex task that requires machines to understand visual patterns, textures, and shapes.

Key Techniques:

- **Convolutional Neural Networks (CNNs):** These are deep learning models specifically designed for image recognition. CNNs can automatically learn hierarchical features from raw image data.
- **Object Detection:** Identifying and locating specific objects within an image.
- **Image Segmentation:** Dividing an image into meaningful regions, each corresponding to a specific object or part of an object.
- **Image Classification:** Categorizing an entire image into a specific class or label.

Real-world Applications:

- **Self-driving Cars:** Identifying pedestrians, traffic signs, and other vehicles.
- **Medical Image Analysis:** Detecting diseases like cancer in X-rays and MRIs.

- **Facial Recognition:** Unlocking smartphones, identifying individuals in security systems.
- **Retail:** Inventory management, visual search, and personalized recommendations.

Speech Recognition

Speech recognition, also known as automatic speech recognition (ASR), is the process of converting spoken language into written text.It involves analyzing audio signals and identifying the words and phrases spoken.

Key Techniques:

- **Acoustic Modeling:** Converting audio signals into a sequence of phonetic units.
- **Language Modeling:** Predicting the most likely sequence of words based on context.
- **Decoding:** Combining acoustic and language models to produce the most probable transcription.

Real-world Applications:

- **Virtual Assistants:** Interacting with devices using voice commands.
- **Transcription Services:** Automatically transcribing audio and video content.
- **Voice Search:** Searching for information using voice queries.
- **Accessibility:** Enabling people with disabilities to interact with technology.

The Future of Image and Speech Recognition

The future of image and speech recognition is bright, with ongoing research and development pushing the boundaries of what's possible. We can expect to see even more sophisticated and accurate systems that can understand and respond to complex visual and auditory information.

Medical Diagnosis: Artificial Intelligence (AI) is rapidly transforming the field of medicine, particularly in the realm of medical diagnosis. By analyzing vast amounts of medical data, AI algorithms can assist healthcare professionals in making more accurate and timely diagnoses.

Key Techniques

- **Machine Learning:**

    - **Supervised Learning:** Trains models on labeled data to classify diseases based on symptoms, medical history, and test results.
    - **Unsupervised Learning:** Identifies patterns in unlabeled data to uncover hidden insights and anomalies.

- **Deep Learning:**

    - **Convolutional Neural Networks (CNNs):** Analyze medical images like X-rays, MRIs, and CT scans to detect abnormalities.
    - **Recurrent Neural Networks (RNNs):** Process sequential data, such as electrocardiograms (ECGs) and electroencephalograms (EEGs), to identify irregularities.

Applications in Medical Diagnosis

- **Cancer Detection:** AI algorithms can analyze medical images to detect early signs of cancer, such as tumors in mammograms or lung nodules in CT scans.
- **Disease Diagnosis:** AI can help diagnose a wide range of diseases, including heart disease, diabetes, and neurodegenerative disorders.
- **Drug Discovery:** AI can accelerate drug discovery by analyzing vast amounts of biological data to identify potential drug targets.

- **Personalized Medicine**: AI can analyze a patient's genetic information and medical history to develop personalized treatment plans.

Benefits of AI in Medical Diagnosis

- **Improved Accuracy**: AI algorithms can often outperform human experts in detecting subtle patterns and anomalies in medical data.
- **Faster Diagnosis**: AI can analyze large datasets quickly, leading to faster diagnoses and treatment initiation.
- **Reduced Cost**: AI-powered tools can reduce healthcare costs by streamlining processes and improving efficiency.
- **Enhanced Patient Care**: AI can help identify high-risk patients and provide personalized care plans.

Challenges and Ethical Considerations

- **Data Quality and Bias**: AI models rely on high-quality data. Biased data can lead to biased models, which may perpetuate healthcare disparities.
- **Explainability**: AI models can be complex and difficult to interpret, making it challenging to understand their decision-making process.
- **Regulatory Hurdles**: The adoption of AI in healthcare requires careful regulatory oversight to ensure patient safety and privacy.

As AI continues to advance, its potential to revolutionize medical diagnosis is immense. By addressing the challenges and ethical considerations, we can harness the power of AI to improve patient outcomes and transform healthcare delivery.

Financial Forecasting: Financial forecasting, particularly in the context of stock market trends, is a complex endeavor that has captivated investors and analysts for decades. While it's impossible to predict the market with absolute certainty, advanced techniques and data-driven approaches have significantly improved our ability to make informed predictions.

Key Techniques for Financial Forecasting:

1. **Technical Analysis:**

   - **Chart Patterns:** Identifying recurring patterns in price charts to predict future trends.
   - **Technical Indicators:** Using mathematical formulas to analyze market data, such as moving averages, RSI, and Bollinger Bands.

2. **Fundamental Analysis:**

   - **Financial Statements:** Evaluating a company's financial health through its income statement, balance sheet, and cash flow statement.
   - **Economic Indicators:** Analyzing macroeconomic factors like GDP, inflation, and interest rates.
   - **Industry Analysis:** Assessing the competitive landscape and industry trends.

3. **Quantitative Analysis:**

   - **Statistical Models:** Employing statistical techniques like time series analysis, regression analysis, and ARIMA models to forecast future values.
   - **Machine Learning:** Leveraging algorithms to learn from historical data and make predictions.

Challenges and Considerations:

- **Market Volatility:** The stock market is inherently volatile, influenced by various factors like economic events, geopolitical tensions, and investor sentiment.

- **Data Quality and Quantity:** The accuracy of forecasts depends on the quality and quantity of data used.
- **Model Complexity:** Complex models may require significant computational resources and expertise to implement and interpret.
- **Overfitting:** Models that are too complex may overfit the training data, leading to poor performance on new data.

The Role of AI and Machine Learning:

Artificial intelligence and machine learning have revolutionized financial forecasting by enabling the analysis of vast amounts of data and the identification of complex patterns. Some key applications include:

- **Predictive Analytics:** Forecasting future stock prices and market trends.
- **Sentiment Analysis:** Analyzing news articles, social media posts, and other textual data to gauge market sentiment.
- **Algorithmic Trading:** Developing automated trading systems that execute trades based on predefined rules and algorithms.

While financial forecasting is a challenging task, by combining traditional techniques with advanced analytical tools, investors and analysts can make more informed decisions and improve their investment outcomes. It's important to remember that no method is foolproof, and a diversified investment strategy is crucial to managing risk.

Self-Driving Cars: Self-driving cars, or autonomous vehicles, are rapidly evolving technology that promises to revolutionize transportation. These vehicles use a combination of sensors, cameras, and AI algorithms to perceive their surroundings, make decisions, andcontrol their movement.

Key Components of Self-Driving Cars:

1. **Sensors:**

- **LiDAR (Light Detection and Ranging):** Measures distances to objects using laser beams.
- **Radar:** Detects objects using radio waves.
- **Cameras:** Capture visual information from the environment.
- **Ultrasonic Sensors:** Detect nearby objects using sound waves.

2. **Perception:**

- **Object Detection:** Identifying objects like cars, pedestrians, and traffic signs.
- **Semantic Segmentation:** Classifying different parts of the scene, such as roads, sidewalks, and buildings.
- **Motion Prediction:** Predicting the future movement of other vehicles and pedestrians.

3. **Decision-Making:**

- **Planning:** Determining the best course of action to reach a destination.
- **Control:** Executing the planned actions by controlling the vehicle's steering, acceleration, and braking.

Challenges and Considerations:

- **Sensor Fusion:** Combining information from multiple sensors to create a comprehensive understanding of the environment.
- **Edge Cases:** Handling unexpected situations, such as adverse weather conditions, construction zones, and unusual traffic patterns.
- **Ethical Dilemmas:** Making difficult decisions in life-threatening situations, such as choosing between hitting a pedestrian or swerving into oncoming traffic.
- **Legal and Regulatory Framework:** Developing clear regulations and standards for autonomous vehicles.

- **Public Acceptance:** Overcoming public concerns about safety and reliability.

The Future of Self-Driving Cars:
Despite the challenges, the potential benefits of self-driving cars are significant:

- **Improved Safety:** Reduced accidents caused by human error.
- **Increased Accessibility:** Transportation for people with disabilities.
- **Reduced Traffic Congestion:** Optimized traffic flow.
- **Environmental Benefits:** Reduced carbon emissions.

As technology continues to advance and societal acceptance grows, self-driving cars are poised to transform the way we travel and live.

Machine Learning is revolutionizing various industries, making our lives more efficient and intelligent.

Defining Machine Learning:
Imagine teaching a computer to learn from experience, just like a human does. That's essentially what Machine Learning (ML) is. It's a field of artificial intelligence that empowers computers to learn from data and make decisions or predictions without being explicitly programmed.

Think of it like this: You show a child pictures of cats and dogs. After seeing enough examples, the child learns to distinguish between the two. Similarly, in ML, we feed a computer a massive amount of data (like images of cats and dogs) and it learns to identify patterns and make accurate predictions.

Key Points:

- **Data:** The fuel for ML algorithms. It can be structured (e.g., spreadsheets) or unstructured (e.g., text, images).
- **Algorithms:** The mathematical models that process the data to identify patterns and relationships.

- **Training:** The process of feeding the algorithm with data to learn and improve its performance.
- **Prediction/Decision Making:** Once trained, the model can make predictions or decisions on new, unseen data.

In a nutshell, Machine Learning is about creating intelligent systems that can learn from data and improve their performance over time.

The Evolution of Machine Learning:

The evolution of Machine Learning has been a fascinating journey, marked by significant advancements from simple algorithms to complex neural networks.

Early Beginnings:

- **Perceptrons (1950s-1960s):** These were early neural networks capable of learning simple patterns. While they were limited, they laid the foundation for future developments.
- **Decision Trees (1970s-1980s):** These algorithms used a tree-like structure to make decisions based on a series of questions. They were popular for their interpretability.

The Rise of Neural Networks:

- **Backpropagation (1980s):** This algorithm revolutionized neural networks by enabling them to learn from their mistakes and improve their performance.
- **Deep Learning (2010s):** With increased computing power and larger datasets, deep learning models with multiple layers became capable of tackling complex tasks like image and speech recognition.

Modern Machine Learning:

- **Convolutional Neural Networks (CNNs):** These are specialized neural networks designed for image and video analysis.

- **Recurrent Neural Networks (RNNs):** These networks are well-suited for sequential data like text and time series.
- **Generative Adversarial Networks (GANs):** These networks can generate realistic images, videos, and text.

The Future:

Machine Learning continues to evolve rapidly. We can expect to see further advancements in:

- **Reinforcement Learning:** Training AI agents to make decisions in complex environments.
- **Transfer Learning:** Leveraging knowledge from one task to improve performance on another.
- **Explainable AI:** Making machine learning models more transparent and understandable.

As Machine Learning becomes more sophisticated, it has the potential to revolutionize various industries and shape the future of technology.

Real-world applications of Machine Learning:

Machine Learning has infiltrated various industries, revolutionizing how we live and work. Here are some real-world examples:

Healthcare:

- **Disease Diagnosis:** ML algorithms analyze medical images like X-rays and MRIs to detect diseases like cancer with high accuracy.
- **Drug Discovery:** ML accelerates drug discovery by predicting the efficacy of molecules.
- **Personalized Medicine:** ML algorithms can analyze patient data to recommend personalized treatment plans.

Finance:

- **Fraud Detection:** ML models can identify fraudulent transactions by analyzing patterns in large datasets.
- **Algorithmic Trading:** ML algorithms can automate trading decisions based on market trends and historical data.
- **Credit Scoring:** ML models can assess creditworthiness more accurately.

E-commerce:

- **Recommendation Systems:** ML algorithms analyze user behavior to suggest products or content.
- **Price Optimization:** ML models can optimize pricing strategies to maximize revenue.
- **Customer Segmentation:** ML algorithms can group customers based on their preferences and behavior.

Marketing:

- **Customer Segmentation:** Similar to e-commerce, ML can group customers for targeted marketing campaigns.
- **Sentiment Analysis:** ML models analyze social media and customer reviews to gauge public sentiment.
- **Predictive Analytics:** ML models can forecast future customer behavior to optimize marketing efforts.

Autonomous Vehicles:

- **Self-Driving Cars:** ML algorithms enable cars to perceive their surroundings and make decisions in real-time.
- **Traffic Prediction:** ML models can analyze traffic patterns to optimize routes and reduce congestion.

Entertainment:

- **Content Recommendation:** ML algorithms suggest movies, TV shows, and music based on user preferences.
- **Content Creation:** ML can generate creative content like music and art.

These are just a few examples of how Machine Learning is transforming various industries. As the technology continues to advance, we can expect even more innovative applications in the future.

TWO
GETTING STARTED WITH MACHINE LEARNING

Online Learning Platforms: Your Gateway to Knowledge

The digital age has revolutionized education, making it accessible to anyone with an internet connection. Online learning platforms like Coursera, edX, and Udemy offer a wide range of courses and tutorials on various subjects, from programming and data science to business and humanities.

Key Benefits of Online Learning:

- **Flexibility:** Learn at your own pace and on your own schedule.
- **Accessibility:** Access courses from anywhere in the world.
- **Variety:** Choose from a vast array of courses and specializations.
- **Affordability:** Many courses are free or offered at a fraction of the cost of traditional education.
- **Interactive Learning:** Engage with instructors and fellow learners through forums, quizzes, and projects.

Popular Online Learning Platforms:

- **Coursera:** Offers courses from top universities and institutions worldwide, covering a wide range of subjects.
- **edX:** Provides high-quality courses from leading universities and institutions.
- **Udemy:** Offers a vast selection of courses, many of which are created by industry experts and independent instructors.

How to Choose the Right Course:

1. **Identify Your Goals:** Determine what you want to learn and what skills you want to acquire.
2. **Check the Course Curriculum:** Ensure the course covers the topics you're interested in.
3. **Read Reviews and Ratings:** See what other learners have to say about the course.
4. **Consider the Instructor's Expertise:** Look for instructors with relevant experience and a good teaching style.
5. **Check the Course Format:** Choose a format that suits your learning style (video lectures, quizzes, assignments, etc.).
6. **Consider the Time Commitment:** Estimate the time required to complete the course.

Tips for Effective Online Learning:

- **Create a Dedicated Learning Space:** Set up a quiet and distraction-free environment.
- **Set Realistic Goals:** Break down the course into smaller, manageable tasks.
- **Stay Organized:** Use a calendar or planner to track your progress.
- **Participate Actively:** Engage with other learners and instructors through forums and discussions.
- **Take Notes and Review Regularly:** Reinforce your learning through active note-taking and regular review.

- **Practice Regularly:** Apply what you've learned through practice exercises and projects.

By leveraging online learning platforms and following these tips, you can embark on a journey of continuous learning and skill development.

Python and R:

Python and R are two of the most popular programming languages used in data science and machine learning. They offer a wide range of libraries and tools that make it easy to work with data, build models, and visualize results.

Python:
Why Python?

- **Readability:** Python's syntax is clean and easy to learn, making it accessible to beginners and experienced programmers alike.
- **Versatility:** It can be used for a variety of tasks, including web development, data analysis, machine learning, and scientific computing.
- **Rich Ecosystem:** Python has a vast ecosystem of libraries and frameworks:

  - **NumPy:** For numerical computations.
  - **Pandas:** For data manipulation and analysis.
  - **Matplotlib and Seaborn:** For data visualization.
  - **Scikit-learn:** For machine learning algorithms.
  - **TensorFlow and PyTorch:** For deep learning.

R:
Why R?

- **Statistical Computing:** R is specifically designed for statistical analysis and data visualization.
- **Data Analysis:** It offers powerful data analysis and manipulation capabilities.

- **Data Visualization:** R provides a wide range of packages for creating stunning visualizations.
- **Machine Learning:** R has a strong machine learning ecosystem, including packages like caret, randomForest, and xgboost.

Choosing the Right Language

The choice between Python and R often depends on your specific needs and preferences. Here are some factors to consider:

- **Data Science and Machine Learning:** Both Python and R are excellent choices. Python's versatility and ease of use make it a popular choice for many data scientists.
- **Statistical Computing and Data Analysis:** R is a strong choice due to its statistical capabilities and specialized packages.
- **Web Development:** Python is a more popular choice for web development.
- **Team Preferences and Existing Tools:** Consider the skills and tools already used by your team.

In many cases, it's beneficial to learn both Python and R to maximize your skills and flexibility.

Key Libraries and Frameworks for Machine Learning

TensorFlow

TensorFlow is an open-source platform developed by Google for machine learning and artificial intelligence. It provides a flexible ecosystem of tools, libraries, and resources that enable researchers and developers to build and deploy machine learning models.

Key Features:

- **TensorFlow Core:** A flexible framework for building and deploying machine learning models.
- **Keras:** A high-level API built on top of TensorFlow, providing a user-friendly interface for building neural networks.
- **TensorFlow Lite:** A lightweight solution for deploying models on mobile and embedded devices.

- **TensorFlow Extended (TFX):** A platform for deploying production machine learning pipelines.

PyTorch

PyTorch is a popular open-source machine learning framework known for its flexibility and ease of use. It's particularly well-suited for deep learning research and prototyping.

Key Features:

- **Dynamic Computational Graph:** Allows for flexible and dynamic model architectures.
- **Strong GPU Support:** Enables efficient training of large models on GPUs.
- **PyTorch Lightning:** A high-level interface for training complex deep learning models.
- **TorchServe:** A framework for deploying PyTorch models.

Scikit-learn

Scikit-learn is a powerful machine learning library built on top of NumPy, SciPy, and Matplotlib. It provides a wide range of algorithms for classification, regression, clustering, and other machine learning tasks.

Key Features:

- **User-Friendly Interface:** Easy-to-use API for building and evaluating machine learning models.
- **Comprehensive Algorithms:** Includes a wide range of algorithms, including linear regression, logistic regression, decision trees, random forests, support vector machines, and more.
- **Model Selection and Evaluation:** Provides tools for model selection, hyperparameter tuning, and model evaluation.
- **Data Preprocessing and Feature Engineering:** Offers tools for data cleaning, normalization, and feature engineering.

By mastering these libraries and frameworks, you can effectively build and deploy machine learning models for a wide range of applications.

Cloud Platforms:

Cloud platforms have revolutionized the way we develop, deploy, and scale applications. They offer a wide range of services, including computing power, storage, databases, and machine learning tools.

Here are some of the leading cloud platforms:

Google Cloud Platform (GCP)

- **Strengths:** Strong AI and machine learning capabilities, scalable infrastructure, and a user-friendly interface.
- **Key Services:**

  - Compute Engine: Virtual machines for running applications.
  - App Engine: Platform for building and hosting web applications.
  - Cloud Storage: Scalable object storage.
  - BigQuery: Serverless data warehouse.
  - AI Platform: Tools for building and deploying machine learning models.

Amazon Web Services (AWS)

- **Strengths:** Extensive range of services, robust infrastructure, and a strong global presence.
- **Key Services:**

  - EC2: Elastic Compute Cloud for virtual machines.
  - S3: Simple Storage Service for object storage.
  - RDS: Relational Database Service for databases.
  - Lambda: Serverless computing platform.
  - SageMaker: Fully managed platform for machine learning.

Microsoft Azure

- **Strengths:** Strong integration with Microsoft products, hybrid cloud capabilities, and enterprise-grade security.
- **Key Services:**

  - Virtual Machines: For running virtual machines on Azure.
  - Azure Storage: For storing data in the cloud.
  - Azure SQL Database: Fully managed relational database service.
  - Azure Functions: Serverless computing platform.
  - Azure Machine Learning: Platform for building, training, and deploying machine learning models.

Choosing the Right Cloud Platform

When selecting a cloud platform, consider the following factors:

- **Scalability:** The ability to scale resources up or down to meet changing demands.
- **Performance:** The speed and reliability of the platform's services.
- **Security:** The level of security and compliance offered by the platform.
- **Cost:** The pricing model and cost-effectiveness of the services.
- **Integration:** The ease of integration with existing systems and tools.

By understanding the strengths and weaknesses of each platform, you can make informed decisions to choose the best cloud solution for your specific needs.

THREE
TYPES OF MACHINE LEARNING

Supervised Learning:

Learning from Labeled Data:

Supervised Learning is a type of machine learning where algorithms learn from labeled data. This means that each data point is paired with a corresponding output or target variable. By analyzing these labeled examples, the algorithm learns to make predictions or decisions on new, unseen data.

How it Works:

1. **Data Collection and Labeling:**

   - Gather a dataset of relevant data points.
   - Assign correct labels or categories to each data point. For example, in image classification, you might label images as "cat" or "dog."

2. **Model Training:**

   - The algorithm is fed the labeled data and learns to identify patterns and relationships between the input features and the corresponding labels.

- ○ Through an iterative process, the model adjusts its internal parameters to minimize the error between its predictions and the actual labels.

3. **Model Evaluation:**

   - ○ Once the model is trained, it is tested on a separate set of labeled data to assess its accuracy and performance.
   - ○ Common evaluation metrics include accuracy, precision, recall, and F1-score.

4. **Model Deployment:**

   - ○ The trained model can be deployed to make predictions on new, unlabeled data.

Common Supervised Learning Algorithms:

- **Linear Regression:** Predicts numerical values.
- **Logistic Regression:** Classifies data into categories.
- **Decision Trees:** Makes decisions based on a tree-like structure.
- **Random Forest:** Combines multiple decision trees for improved accuracy.
- **Support Vector Machines (SVM):** Finds optimal decision boundaries.
- **Naive Bayes:** Classifies based on probability theory.
- **K-Nearest Neighbors (KNN):** Classifies based on similarity.

Real-world Applications:

- **Email Spam Filtering:** Classifying emails as spam or not spam.
- **Image Recognition:** Identifying objects in images.
- **Medical Diagnosis:** Predicting diseases based on medical records.
- **Financial Forecasting:** Predicting stock prices or market trends.

By learning from labeled data, supervised learning enables machines to make accurate predictions and decisions, driving innovation in various fields.

Classification and Regression:

In the realm of supervised machine learning, classification and regression are two fundamental tasks. They differ in the type of output they predict.

Classification

- **Predicts categorical values:** The model assigns data points to predefined categories or classes.
- **Output:** Discrete values (e.g., "yes" or "no," "spam" or "not spam," "cat" or "dog").
- **Common Algorithms:**

    ○ Logistic Regression
    ○ Decision Trees
    ○ Random Forest
    ○ Support Vector Machines (SVM)
    ○ Naive Bayes
    ○ K-Nearest Neighbors (KNN)
    ○ Neural Networks

Real-world Examples of Classification:

- **Email Spam Detection:** Classifying emails as spam or not spam.
- **Medical Diagnosis:** Predicting diseases based on symptoms.
- **Image Recognition:** Identifying objects in images.
- **Sentiment Analysis:** Determining the sentiment of text (positive, negative, neutral).

Regression

- **Predicts continuous values:** The model predicts a numerical value.

- **Output:** Continuous values (e.g., house prices, stock prices, temperature).
- **Common Algorithms:**

  - Linear Regression
  - Polynomial Regression
  - Ridge Regression
  - Lasso Regression
  - Support Vector Regression (SVR)
  - Decision Tree Regression
  - Random Forest Regression
  - K-Nearest Neighbors (KNN) Regression
  - Neural Networks

Real-world Examples of Regression:

- **Sales Forecasting:** Predicting future sales based on historical data.
- **Stock Price Prediction:** Forecasting stock prices.
- **Real Estate Price Prediction:** Predicting house prices based on features like size, location, and age.
- **Weather Forecasting:** Predicting temperature and precipitation.

Real-world Examples of Supervised Learning: Spam filters employ supervised learning techniques to distinguish between legitimate emails and spam.

How it works:

1. **Data Collection and Labeling:** A large dataset of emails is collected and labeled as either "spam" or "not spam."
2. **Feature Extraction:** Key features like the sender's email address, subject line, content, and presence of specific keywords are extracted from each email.
3. **Model Training:** A machine learning algorithm, such as Naive Bayes or Support Vector Machines, is trained on the labeled

dataset. The algorithm learns to associate certain features with spam emails.

4. **Prediction:** When a new email arrives, the filter extracts its features and feeds them into the trained model. The model then predicts whether the email is spam or not.

Recommendation Systems

Recommendation systems, commonly found on e-commerce websites and streaming platforms, leverage supervised learning to suggest products or content tailored to individual preferences.

How it works:

1. **Data Collection and Labeling:** User behavior data, such as purchase history, browsing history, and ratings, is collected and labeled with relevant information.
2. **Feature Extraction:** Features like user demographics, product categories, and purchase frequency are extracted from the data.
3. **Model Training:** Collaborative filtering and content-based filtering are common techniques used to train recommendation models. Collaborative filtering analyzes user-item interactions to find similar users and products. Content-based filtering recommendstems similar to those a user has previously interacted with.
4. **Recommendation Generation:** The trained model analyzes a user's profile and generates personalized recommendations.

By effectively utilizing supervised learning, spam filters and recommendation systems enhance user experience and improve business outcomes.

Unsupervised Learning:

Discovering Patterns in Unlabeled Data:

Unsupervised learning is a type of machine learning where algorithms learn from unlabeled data. Unlike supervised learning, there are no predefined categories or labels for the data points. Instead, the algorithm explores the data to discover hidden patterns and structures.

Key Techniques in Unsupervised Learning

1. **Clustering:**

   - **K-Means Clustering:** Divides data into a specified number of clusters based on similarity.
   - **Hierarchical Clustering:** Creates a hierarchy of clusters, starting from individual data points and merging them into larger clusters.
   - **DBSCAN:** Groups together points that are closely packed together (core points) and marks outliers.

2. **Dimensionality Reduction:**

   - **Principal Component Analysis (PCA):** Reduces the dimensionality of data while preserving most of the variance.
   - **t-SNE:** Visualizes high-dimensional data in a lower-dimensional space, often 2D or 3D.

Real-world Applications of Unsupervised Learning

- **Customer Segmentation:** Grouping customers based on their purchasing behavior, demographics, or other relevant factors.
- **Anomaly Detection:** Identifying unusual data points that may indicate errors, fraud, or other anomalies.
- **Feature Engineering:** Creating new features from existing ones to improve the performance of supervised learning models.
- **Topic Modeling:** Discovering underlying topics in a collection of documents.
- **Image and Video Analysis:** Identifying patterns and objects in images and videos without explicit labels.

Example: Customer Segmentation

Imagine an e-commerce company with a large customer base. By applying unsupervised learning techniques, the company can:

1. **Cluster Customers:** Group customers based on their purchasing behavior, demographics, and preferences.
2. **Identify Segments:** Discover distinct customer segments, such as "frequent shoppers," "bargain hunters," or "tech enthusiasts."
3. **Tailored Marketing:** Develop targeted marketing campaigns for each segment, increasing customer satisfaction and sales.

By leveraging the power of unsupervised learning, businesses can gain valuable insights from their data, make informed decisions, and improve their operations.

Clustering and Dimensionality Reduction:

Clustering

Clustering is a technique used to group similar data points together. It's like sorting objects into categories based on their similarities.

Common Clustering Algorithms:

- **K-Means Clustering:** Divides data into a specified number (K) of clusters.
- **Hierarchical Clustering:** Creates a hierarchy of clusters, starting from individual data points and merging them into larger clusters.
- **DBSCAN:** Groups together points that are closely packed together (core points) and marks outliers.

Applications of Clustering:

- **Customer Segmentation:** Grouping customers based on their purchasing behavior.
- **Image Segmentation:** Dividing images into regions with similar characteristics.
- **Anomaly Detection:** Identifying unusual data points.

Dimensionality Reduction

Dimensionality reduction is a technique used to reduce the number of features in a dataset. It's helpful when dealing with high-dimensional data, which can be challenging to visualize and analyze.

Common Dimensionality Reduction Techniques:

- **Principal Component Analysis (PCA):** Identifies the principal components of variation in the data and projects the data onto a lower-dimensional space.
- **t-SNE:** A nonlinear technique that preserves local structure in the data.
- **Linear Discriminant Analysis (LDA):** Reduces dimensionality while maximizing class separability.

Applications of Dimensionality Reduction:

- **Data Visualization:** Visualizing high-dimensional data in 2D or 3D.
- **Feature Extraction:** Creating new features that capture the most important information in the data.
- **Noise Reduction:** Removing irrelevant features that can noise the model.

Why are Clustering and Dimensionality Reduction Important?

- **Improved Performance:** By reducing the number of features, we can improve the performance of machine learning algorithms.
- **Reduced Computational Cost:** Fewer features mean faster training and prediction times.
- **Better Visualization:** Visualizing high-dimensional data can be challenging. Dimensionality reduction techniques allow us to visualize data in lower-dimensional spaces.
- **Discovering Hidden Patterns:** Clustering can help uncover hidden patterns and structures in data.

By understanding and applying clustering and dimensionality reduction techniques, we can gain valuable insights from complex data and make better decisions.

Customer Segmentation

Customer segmentation involves grouping customers into distinct segments based on shared characteristics. Unsupervised learning techniques, such as clustering, can be used to identify these segments without prior knowledge of customer labels.

How it works:

1. **Data Collection:** Collect customer data, including demographic information, purchase history, browsing behavior, and other relevant attributes.
2. **Feature Extraction:** Extract relevant features from the collected data.
3. **Clustering:** Apply a clustering algorithm, like K-Means or Hierarchical Clustering, to group similar customers together.
4. **Segment Analysis:** Analyze the characteristics of each cluster to identify distinct customer segments.

Benefits of Customer Segmentation:

- **Targeted Marketing:** Develop tailored marketing campaigns for each segment.
- **Product Development:** Design products and services that cater to specific customer needs.
- **Improved Customer Experience:** Provide personalized experiences to enhance customer satisfaction.

Anomaly Detection

Anomaly detection involves identifying data points that deviate significantly from the norm. Unsupervised learning techniques can be used to identify these outliers without explicit labels.

How it works:

1. **Data Collection:** Collect a dataset of normal data points.
2. **Feature Extraction:** Extract relevant features from the data.
3. **Model Training:** Train an unsupervised learning model, such as a clustering or density-based algorithm, on the normal data.
4. **Anomaly Detection:** Identify data points that are significantly different from the clusters or have low density.

Applications of Anomaly Detection:

- **Fraud Detection:** Identify fraudulent transactions in financial systems.
- **Network Security:** Detect malicious network traffic.
- **Manufacturing:** Identify defective products or equipment failures.
- **Healthcare:** Detect unusual patterns in patient data that may indicate health issues.

By effectively applying unsupervised learning techniques, businesses can gain valuable insights from their data, make informed decisions, and improve their operations.

Reinforcement Learning:

Learning Through Trial and Error:

Reinforcement Learning is a type of machine learning where an agent learns to make decisions by interacting withan environment. It's essentially learning through trial and error, much like how a child learns to walk or a dog learns to fetch.

Key Components of Reinforcement Learning:

- **Agent:** The decision-maker, such as a robot or a software program.
- **Environment:** The world in which the agent operates.
- **State:** The current situation or condition of the environment.
- **Action:** The choice made by the agent to influence the environment.

- **Reward:** A numerical value assigned to a state-action pair, indicating the desirability of a particular action in a given state.

How it Works:

1. **Exploration and Exploitation:** The agent explores different actions to discover which ones lead to higher rewards. It also exploits known good actions to maximize immediate rewards.
2. **Learning:** The agent learns from its experiences, associating actions with rewards. Over time, it develops a strategy to maximize cumulative rewards.
3. **Policy Improvement:** The agent continually refines its policy, which is a mapping from states to actions. This improvement is driven by the feedback from the environment.

Real-world Applications:

- **Game Playing:** AI agents have mastered complex games like Chess, Go, and Dota 2 through reinforcement learning.
- **Robotics:** Robots can learn to perform tasks like walking, grasping objects, and navigating environments.
- **Autonomous Vehicles:** Self-driving cars can learn to make safe and efficient driving decisions.
- **Finance:** Reinforcement learning can be used to optimize trading strategies and risk management.

By learning from its mistakes and successes, reinforcement learning agents can achieve remarkable performance in a wide range of tasks, pushing the boundaries of artificial intelligence.

Agent-Environment Interaction:

Agent-environment interaction is the fundamental process in reinforcement learning. It's a continuous loop where an agent interacts with an environment, takes actions, receives feedback in the form of rewards or penalties, and learns to make better decisions over time.

The Cycle of Interaction:

1. **Perception:** The agent perceives the current state of the environment. This state can be a simple observation or a complex representation of the world.
2. **Action:** Based on its perception, the agent selects an action from a set of possible actions. This action can be a physical movement, a decision, or a command.
3. **Execution:** The agent executes the chosen action in the environment.
4. **Reward:** The environment provides a reward or penalty to the agent, indicating the immediate consequence of the action.
5. **State Transition:** The environment transitions to a new state as a result of the agent's action.

Key Concepts:
State:
The global environment faces a multitude of pressing challenges, many of which are interconnected and exacerbated by human activities. Here's a brief overview of the current situation:
Climate Change

- **Rising Global Temperatures:** The Earth's average temperature is steadily increasing, leading to more frequent and severe heatwaves, droughts, and floods.
- **Melting Ice Caps and Sea-Level Rise:** This poses a significant threat to coastal cities and island nations.
- **Ocean Acidification:** Increased CO_2 absorption by oceans is harming marine ecosystems.

Biodiversity Loss

- **Habitat Destruction:** Deforestation and urbanization are destroying natural habitats.

- **Overexploitation:** Overfishing, hunting, and illegal wildlife trade are depleting species populations.
- **Pollution:** Air, water, and land pollution are harming ecosystems and wildlife.

Pollution

- **Air Pollution:** Poor air quality, primarily caused by fossil fuel combustion, contributes to respiratory diseases and climate change.
- **Water Pollution:** Industrial and agricultural runoff, as well as plastic pollution, are contaminating water bodies.
- **Land Pollution:** Improper waste disposal and chemical use are degrading soil quality.

Resource Depletion

- **Fossil Fuels:** Depleting reserves and environmental concerns are driving the need for renewable energy sources.
- **Water Scarcity:** Growing populations and unsustainable water use are leading to water shortages.
- **Deforestation:** Forests are being cleared for agriculture, timber, and other purposes.

Solutions and Hope

Despite these challenges, there is hope. Many individuals, organizations, and governments are working to address these issues:

- **Renewable Energy:** Transitioning to clean energy sources like solar, wind, and hydro power.
- **Sustainable Agriculture:** Adopting practices that minimize environmental impact.
- **Conservation Efforts:** Protecting endangered species and their habitats.

- **Circular Economy:** Reducing waste and promoting recycling.
- **International Cooperation:** Collaborating on global environmental issues.

By taking collective action and embracing sustainable practices, we can mitigate the negative impacts of human activities and ensure a healthier planet for future generations.

Action:

In the realm of artificial intelligence (AI), an action represents a specific behavior or decision made by an agent to influence its environment. It's the tangible output of an agent's decision-making process.

Key Concepts:

- **Agent:** An entity that can perceive its environment and take actions to achieve its goals.
- **Environment:** The external setting in which the agent operates.
- **State:** The current condition of the environment.
- **Policy:** A strategy that maps states to actions.

Types of Actions:

1. **Discrete Actions:** Actions that are finite and well-defined. For instance, in a chess game, the possible actions are the different moves a player can make.
2. **Continuous Actions:** Actions that can take on any value within a specific range. For example, controlling the steering angle of a self-driving car.

Action Selection:

The process of choosing the best action is crucial in AI. Several techniques are employed:

- **Reinforcement Learning:** Agents learn to make optimal decisions through trial and error, receiving rewards or penalties for their actions.

- **Rule-Based Systems**: Agents follow predefined rules to determine actions.
- **Search Algorithms**: Agents explore different action sequences to find the best solution.

Real-World Examples:

- **Self-driving cars**: Actions like accelerating, braking, and steering.
- **Game-playing AI**: Actions like moving pieces on a chessboard or choosing a card in a poker game.
- **Robotics**: Actions like picking up objects, moving limbs, or navigating a maze.
- **Chatbots**: Actions like responding to user queries, providing information, or completing tasks.

In essence, actions are the building blocks of intelligent behavior. By understanding and effectively implementing actions, AI agents can achieve complex goals and interact intelligently with the world.

Reward:

A reward, in the context of reinforcement learning, is a numerical value assigned to a state-action pair. It signifies the immediate benefit or penalty an agent receives for performing a specific action in a particular state. Rewards are essential for guiding the agent's learning process and shaping its behavior.

Key Points:

- **State-Action Pair:** A combination of a specific state the agent is in and the action it takes in that state.
- **Numerical Value:** The reward can be positive, negative, or zero.
- **Desirability:** A positive reward indicates a desirable action, while a negative reward indicates an undesirable action.

Role of Rewards in Reinforcement Learning:

- **Learning Signal:** Rewards serve as a feedback signal, informing the agent about the quality of its actions.
- **Goal Orientation:** Rewards are used to define the agent's goals. The agent learns to maximize the cumulative reward over time.
- **Policy Optimization:** The agent's policy, which maps states to actions, is optimized to maximize the expected cumulative reward.

Types of Rewards:

1. **Sparse Rewards:** Rewards are infrequent and often only given at the end of a task. This makes learning challenging as the agent must explore the environment to discover rewarding states.
2. **Dense Rewards:** Rewards are provided frequently, guiding the agent's learning process more directly.

Reward Shaping: Reward shaping is a technique used to modify the reward function to accelerate learning. It involves adding additional rewards or penalties to guide the agent towards desired behaviors.

Challenges in Reward Design:

- **Reward Sparsity:** Sparse rewards can make learning inefficient.
- **Reward Hacking:** Agents may find unintended ways to maximize rewards, leading to suboptimal behavior.
- **Reward Misspecification:** Poorly designed reward functions can lead to undesirable behavior.

By carefully designing reward functions, reinforcement learning agents can learn to make optimal decisions and achieve complex goals.

Policy:

A policy in reinforcement learning is a strategy that maps states to actions. It essentially defines the behavior of an agent in a given environment. In simpler terms, it's a rulebook that tells the agent what action to take in a given state.

Key Points:

- **State-Action Mapping:** A policy associates each possible state of the environment with a specific action.
- **Decision-Making:** The agent uses the policy to make decisions, aiming to maximize its cumulative reward.
- **Optimization:** The goal of reinforcement learning is to find the optimal policy, which yields the highest expected return.

Types of Policies:

1. **Deterministic Policy:** For a given state, the policy always outputs the same action.
2. **Stochastic Policy:** The policy outputs a probability distribution over actions, indicating the likelihood of taking each action in a given state.

Policy Evaluation and Improvement:

- **Policy Evaluation:** Assessing the value of a given policy by calculating the expected return for each state.
- **Policy Improvement:** Finding a new policy that yields a higher expected return than the current policy.

Popular Policy Optimization Algorithms:

- **Policy Gradient Methods:** Directly optimize the policy parameters to maximize the expected return.
- **Actor-Critic Methods:** Combine policy gradient methods with value function estimation.

- **Proximal Policy Optimization (PPO):** A powerful algorithm that balances exploration and exploitation.

Real-world Applications:

- **Robotics:** Controlling robot arms to perform tasks.
- **Game AI:** Developing AI agents for games like chess, Go, and Dota 2.
- **Autonomous Vehicles:** Making driving decisions in real-time.
- **Recommendation Systems:** Personalizing recommendations based on user preferences.

By understanding and effectively implementing policies, reinforcement learning agents can learn to make optimal decisions and achieve complex goals.

Value Function:

A value function in reinforcement learning is a mathematical function that estimates the expected future reward from a given state. It provides an evaluation of how good it is for an agent to be in a particular state.

Key Points:

- **Expected Future Reward:** The value function predicts the total reward the agent can expect to accumulate in the future, starting from that state and following a specific policy.
- **State Evaluation:** It helps the agent assess the long-term consequences of its actions.
- **Policy Improvement:** By estimating the value of different states, the agent can improve its policy by choosing actions that lead to states with higher values.

Types of Value Functions:

1. **State Value Function (V):**

- ◦ Estimates the expected return starting from a given state and following a specific policy.
- ◦ It's denoted as V(s), where s is a state.

2. **State-Action Value Function (Q):**

- ◦ Estimates the expected return starting from a given state, taking a specific action, and then following a specific policy.
- ◦ It's denoted as Q(s, a), where s is a state and a is an action.

Value Function Estimation:

- **Dynamic Programming:** A mathematical technique used to solve optimization problems, including value function estimation.
- **Monte Carlo Methods:** Statistical methods used to estimate the value function by sampling episodes and calculating the average return.
- **Temporal Difference (TD) Learning:** A combination of dynamic programming and Monte Carlo methods, which updates value function estimates based on temporal differences between successive states.

Importance of Value Functions:

- **Policy Evaluation:** Assessing the quality of a given policy.
- **Policy Improvement:** Finding better policies by maximizing the value function.
- **Decision Making:** Guiding the agent's decision-making process by selecting actions that lead to states with higher values.

By understanding and effectively estimating value functions, reinforcement learning agents can learn to make optimal decisions and achieve their goals.

Example:

- **Agent:** The self-driving car.
- **Environment:** The road, traffic, pedestrians, and other vehicles.
- **State:** The current position and speed of the car, the positions and speeds of other vehicles, traffic lights, and road signs.
- **Action:** Steering, accelerating, or braking.
- **Reward:** Positive rewards for reaching the destination safely and efficiently, negative rewards for accidents or traffic violations.

Through continuous interaction with the environment, the self-driving car learns to make optimal decisions to navigate safely and efficiently.

By understanding the dynamics of agent-environment interaction, we can design intelligent agents that can learn complex behaviors and solve challenging problems.

Self-Driving Cars

Self-driving cars rely on reinforcement learning to navigate complex road conditions and make safe driving decisions.

How it works:

1. **Environment:** The car's surroundings, including roads, traffic, pedestrians, and other vehicles.
2. **Agent:** The self-driving car's AI system.
3. **State:** The car's current position, speed, and the surrounding environment.
4. **Action:** Steering, accelerating, or braking.
5. **Reward:** Positive rewards for safe driving, negative rewards for accidents or traffic violations.

The AI system learns from millions of miles of simulated driving data, as well as real-world driving experiences. Through trial and error, it develops the ability to make safe and efficient driving decisions.

Game-Playing AI

Reinforcement learning has been successfully applied to create AI agents that can master complex games like Chess, Go, and Dota

2.

How it works:

1. **Environment:** The game board and rules.
2. **Agent:** The AI player.
3. **State:** The current configuration of the game board.
4. **Action:** A legal move in the game.
5. **Reward:** Positive rewards for winning the game, negative rewards for losing.

The AI agent learns by playing countless games against itself or other AI agents. It analyzes the outcomes of different moves and adjusts its strategy to maximize its chances of winning.

Benefits of Reinforcement Learning:

- **Adaptability:** Reinforcement learning agents can adapt to changing environments and learn new strategies.
- **Exploration and Exploitation:** The ability to balance exploration (trying new actions) and exploitation (using known good actions).
- **Continuous Learning:** Reinforcement learning agents can continually improve their performance over time.

By leveraging the power of reinforcement learning, we can develop intelligent systems that can solve complex problems and make optimal decisions in dynamic environments.

FOUR
KEY MACHINE LEARNING ALGORITHMS

Linear Regression:

Linear regression is a statistical method used to model the relationship between a dependent variable and one or more independent variables. It's a fundamental technique in machine learning for predicting numerical values.

The Model

A simple linear regression model with one independent variable can be represented as:

$y = mx + b$

Where:

- y: The dependent variable (the value we want to predict)
- x: The independent variable (the input feature)
- m: The slope of the line
- b: The y-intercept

For multiple independent variables, the equation becomes:

$y = b_0 + b_1 x_1 + b_2 x_2 + \ldots + b_n x_n$

Where:

- y: The dependent variable
- x1, x2, ..., xn: The independent variables
- b0, b1, ..., bn: The model coefficients

How it Works:

1. **Data Collection:** Gather data with both independent and dependent variables.
2. **Model Training:**

   - Use an algorithm like Ordinary Least Squares (OLS) to find the best-fitting line (or hyperplane in higher dimensions) that minimizes the sum of squared errors between the predicted and actual values.

1. **Prediction:**

   - Once the model is trained, it can be used to predict the value of the dependent variable for new, unseen data points.

Example: Predicting House Prices

Suppose we want to predict house prices based on features like square footage, number of bedrooms, and location. We can use linear regression to model the relationship between these features and the house price.

Steps:

1. **Data Collection:** Gather data on house prices, square footage, number of bedrooms, location, etc.
2. **Data Preprocessing:** Clean and preprocess the data to handle missing values and outliers.
3. **Model Training:** Train a linear regression model on the prepared data.

4. **Model Evaluation:** Evaluate the model's performance using metrics like Mean Squared Error (MSE) or Root Mean Squared Error (RMSE).
5. **Prediction:** Use the trained model to predict the price of a new house given its features.

Visualization:

Linear regression is a powerful tool for understanding relationships between variables and making numerical predictions. However, it's important to remember that it assumes a linear relationship between the variables. In real-world scenarios, relationships might be more complex, and other techniques like polynomial regression or machine learning models might be more suitable.

Logistic Regression:

Logistic regression is a statistical method used to model the probability of a binary outcome. It's a widely used technique in machine learning for classification tasks.

The Model

While linear regression predicts a continuous numerical value, logistic regression predicts the probability of a binary outcome (e.g., 0 or 1, yes or no). It uses a logistic function (sigmoid function) to map the input values to a probability between 0 and 1.

The logistic function is defined as:

$P(y=1|x) = 1 / (1 + \exp(-z))$

Where:

- $P(y=1|x)$: Probability of the positive class given the input x
- z: Linear combination of input features and weights: $z = w0 + w1*x1 + w2*x2 + \ldots + wn*xn$

How it Works:

1. **Data Collection:** Gather data with both input features and binary class labels.

2. **Model Training:**

   - Use an optimization algorithm like gradient descent to find the optimal weights w that minimize the loss function (e.g., cross-entropy loss).

3. **Prediction:**

   - For a new data point, calculate the probability using the logistic function.
   - If the probability is above a certain threshold (e.g., 0.5), classify it as the positive class, otherwise, the negative class.

Example: Email Spam Detection

Consider the task of classifying emails as spam or not spam. We can use logistic regression to model the probability of an email being spam based on features like the presence of certain words, the sender's email address, and the subject line.

Steps:

1. **Data Collection:** Gather a dataset of emails labeled as spam or not spam.
2. **Feature Extraction:** Extract relevant features from each email, such as word frequency, sender's domain, and the presence of specific keywords.
3. **Model Training:** Train a logistic regression model on the extracted features and labels.
4. **Prediction:** For a new email, extract its features and feed them into the trained model to predict whether it's spam or not.

Key Points:

- Logistic regression is a versatile technique for binary classification problems.

- It can be extended to multi-class classification problems using techniques like one-vs-rest or softmax regression.
- It's interpretable, as the coefficients of the model can be analyzed to understand the impact of each feature.
- It's relatively simple to implement and computationally efficient.

By understanding the principles of logistic regression, you can effectively apply it to a wide range of classification tasks, from medical diagnosis to financial fraud detection.

Decision Trees:

Decision Trees are a popular machine learning algorithm used for both classification and regression tasks. They mimic human decision-making bycreating a tree-like model of decisions and their possible consequences.

How a Decision Tree Works:

1. **Root Node:** This is the starting point of the tree.
2. **Internal Nodes:** These nodes represent features or attributes used to make decisions.
3. **Branches:** Each internal node has branches leading to child nodes.
4. **Leaf Nodes:**

These are the end points of the tree and represent the final decision or prediction.

Decision-Making Process:

1. **Feature Selection:** At each internal node, an algorithm selects the best feature to split the data.
2. **Splitting:** The data is split into subsets based on the selected feature's values.
3. **Recursion:** The process is repeated for each subset until a stopping criterion is met (e.g., maximum depth, minimum number of samples).

Advantages of Decision Trees:

- **Interpretability:** Decision trees are easy to understand and visualize.
- **Handles both numerical and categorical data:** Decision trees can handle both types of data.
- **Non-parametric:** They don't assume any underlying distribution of the data.
- **Feature Importance:** The algorithm can identify the most important features.

Disadvantages of Decision Trees:

- **Overfitting:** Decision trees can be prone to overfitting, especially with deep trees.
- **Sensitivity to Noise:** Noise in the data can lead to suboptimal splits.

Example: Predicting Loan Approval

Suppose we want to predict whether a loan application will be approved or rejected based on features like income, credit score, and loan amount. A decision tree might look like this:

Random Forest:

Random Forest is a powerful machine learning algorithm that combines multiple decision trees to make more accurate predictions. It's an ensemble method that reduces overfitting and improves generalization.

How it Works:

1. **Random Forest Creation:**

   ○ **Multiple Decision Trees:** A large number of decision trees are created.
   ○ **Random Feature Selection:** At each node of a decision tree, a random subset of features is considered for splitting. This

helps to reduce correlation between trees.

- **Bagging:** Each decision tree is trained on a random subset of the training data, drawn with replacement. This technique, called bagging (Bootstrap Aggregating), reduces variance and improves generalization.

2. **Prediction:**

- To make a prediction, each decision tree in the forest votes for a class or a value.
- The final prediction is determined by a majority vote or averaging the predictions of all trees.

Advantages of Random Forest:

- **High Accuracy:** By combining multiple trees, random forests often achieve high accuracy.
- **Robustness to Overfitting:** Random feature selection and bagging help reduce overfitting.
- **Handles Missing Values:** Random forests can handle missing values effectively.
- **Feature Importance:** It can provide feature importance scores, which can be useful for feature selection and understanding the model.
- **Versatility:** Can be used for both classification and regression tasks.

Applications of Random Forest:

- **Predictive Modeling:** Predicting customer churn, stock prices, or loan defaults.
- **Image Classification:** Classifying images into different categories.
- **Medical Diagnosis:** Predicting diseases based on medical data.
- **Fraud Detection:** Identifying fraudulent transactions.

In summary, random forests are a powerful and versatile machine learning algorithm that can handle complex datasets and produce accurate predictions. By combining multiple decision trees and reducing overfitting, they provide a robust and reliable solution for many machine learning problems.

Support Vector Machines (SVM):

Support Vector Machines (SVM) are a powerful machine learning algorithm used for both classification and regression tasks. They are particularly effective in high-dimensional spaces and can handle complex classification problems.

The Core Idea

SVM aims to find the optimal hyperplane that separates the data points into different classes. This hyperplane is chosen such that it maximizes the margin between the closest data points of different classes. These data points, known as support vectors, play a crucial role in defining the decision boundary.

Types of SVMs

1. **Linear SVM:**

   - Used for linearly separable data.
   - Finds a hyperplane that maximizes the margin between the two classes.

2. **Kernel SVM:**

   - Used for non-linearly separable data.
   - Maps the data into a higher-dimensional space where it becomes linearly separable.
   - Common kernels include:

     - **Polynomial Kernel:** Maps data to a polynomial space.
     - **Radial Basis Function (RBF) Kernel:** Maps data to an infinite-dimensional space.

Advantages of SVM:

- **Effective in high-dimensional spaces:** SVMs can handle high-dimensional data without overfitting.
- **Versatile:** Can be used for both classification and regression tasks.
- **Robust to outliers:** SVMs are less sensitive to outliers compared to other algorithms.
- **Good generalization performance:** SVMs often achieve high accuracy.

Disadvantages of SVM:

- **Computational cost:** Training SVMs can be computationally expensive, especially for large datasets.
- **Sensitivity to hyperparameters:** The choice of kernel and hyperparameters can significantly impact performance.
- **Less interpretable:** Compared to decision trees, SVMs are less interpretable.

Applications of SVM:

- **Image classification:** Classifying images into different categories.
- **Text classification:** Classifying text documents into different categories (e.g., spam or not spam).
- **Bioinformatics:** Predicting protein structures and identifying disease-related genes.
- **Financial analysis:** Detecting fraudulent transactions.

By understanding the core concepts of SVM and its variants, you can effectively apply this powerful algorithm to various machine learning tasks.

Naive Bayes:

Naive Bayes is a simple yet powerful probabilistic classification algorithm based on Bayes' theorem. It assumes that features are independent, which is why it's called "naive."

Bayes' Theorem

Bayes' theorem states:

P(A|B) = P(B|A) * P(A) / P(B)

In the context of machine learning, this can be interpreted as:

P(Class|Features) = P(Features|Class) * P(Class) / P(Features)

How Naive Bayes Works:

1. **Feature Independence Assumption:**

   - Naive Bayes assumes that features are independent of each other given the class label. This simplifies the calculations.

2. **Probability Calculation:**

   - Calculate the probability of each class given the input features using Bayes' theorem.
   - The class with the highest probability is assigned to the input data point.

3. **Classification:**

   - The input data point is classified based on the calculated probabilities.

Advantages of Naive Bayes:

- **Simple and Efficient:** Easy to implement and computationally efficient.
- **Handles Missing Values:** Can handle missing values by ignoring features with missing values during probability calculations.
- **Effective for Text Classification:** Works well for text classification tasks like spam filtering and sentiment analysis.

Disadvantages of Naive Bayes:

- **Feature Independence Assumption:** The assumption of feature independence can be violated in real-world scenarios, affecting the accuracy of the model.
- **Zero-Probability Problem:** If a feature value doesn't appear in the training data, the probability of that feature given a class becomes zero, which can lead to incorrect predictions. This can be addressed using techniques like Laplace smoothing.

Applications of Naive Bayes:

- **Text Classification:** Spam filtering, sentiment analysis, document categorization.
- **Medical Diagnosis:** Predicting diseases based on symptoms.
- **Recommendation Systems:** Recommending products or content.

Naive Bayes is a versatile algorithm that can be applied to various classification tasks. While its simplicity and efficiency make it a popular choice, it's important to be aware of its limitations and consider more complex models when necessary.

K-Nearest Neighbors (KNN):

K-Nearest Neighbors (KNN) is a simple yet effective supervised machine learning algorithm used for both classification and regression tasks. Itclassifies data points based on the majority vote of theirk nearest neighbors.

How KNN Works:

1. **Calculate Distance:**

   - For each data point in the training set, calculate the distance to the query point. Common distance metrics include Euclidean distance and Manhattan distance.

2. **Select Nearest Neighbors:**

   ○ Identify the k nearest neighbors to the query point based on the calculated distances.

3. **Classification (for classification tasks):**

   ○ Determine the most frequent class label among the k nearest neighbors.

4. **Regression (for regression tasks):**

   ○ Calculate the average value of the target variable for the k nearest neighbors.

Key Parameters in KNN:

- **k:** The number of neighbors to consider. Choosing the optimal value of k is crucial. A small value of k can be sensitive to noise, while a large value can smooth out decision boundaries but might lead to overfitting.
- **Distance Metric:** The choice of distance metric (e.g., Euclidean, Manhattan, Minkowski) can impact the performance of the algorithm.

Advantages of KNN:

- **Simple to understand and implement.**
- **No explicit training phase.**
- **Versatile:** Can be used for both classification and regression tasks.
- **Effective for low-dimensional data.**

Disadvantages of KNN:

- **Computational Cost:** Can be computationally expensive for large datasets, especially during the prediction phase.
- **Sensitive to the Choice of k:** The choice of k can significantly impact the performance.
- **Curse of Dimensionality:** Can be less effective in high-dimensional spaces, as distance calculations become less meaningful.

Applications of KNN:

- **Recommendation Systems:** Recommending products or content based on similar items or users.
- **Image Classification:** Classifying images based on visual features.
- **Anomaly Detection:** Identifying outliers or anomalies in data.

KNN is a versatile algorithm that can be applied to various machine learning tasks. By carefully selecting the value of k and considering the distance metric, you can achieve good performance, especially for smaller datasets with clear decision boundaries.

Neural Networks:

Neural Networks are a class of machine learning algorithms inspired by the structure and function of the human brain. They are composed of[1] interconnected nodes called neurons, organized in layers.

Basic Structure of a Neural Network:

1. **Input Layer:** Receives input data.
2. **Hidden Layers:** Process the input data through multiple layers of interconnected neurons.
3. **Output Layer:** Produces the final output, such as a classification or regression prediction.

How Neural Networks Work:

1. **Forward Propagation:**

   - Input data is fed into the input layer.
   - The input is processed by the hidden layers, where each neuron performs a weighted sum of its inputs and applies an activation function.
   - The output layer produces the final prediction.

2. **Backpropagation:**

   - The error between the predicted output and the actual output is calculated.
   - The error is propagated backward through the network, adjusting the weights and biases of each neuron.
   - This process is repeated iteratively until the model converges.

Types of Neural Networks:

1. **Feedforward Neural Networks:** Information flows in one direction, from the input layer to the output layer.
2. **Convolutional Neural Networks (CNNs):** Specialized for image and video data, CNNs use convolutional layers to extract features from the input data.
3. **Recurrent Neural Networks (RNNs):** Designed to process sequential data, such as time series or text.
4. **Generative Adversarial Networks (GANs):** Comprised of two networks, a generator and a discriminator, that compete to generate realistic data.

Advantages of Neural Networks:

- **Powerful:** Can learn complex patterns in data.
- **Flexible:** Can be applied to a wide range of tasks, including image and speech recognition, natural language processing, and more.

- **Adaptability:** Can adapt to new data and improve performance over time.

Disadvantages of Neural Networks:

- **Computational Cost:** Training large neural networks can be computationally expensive.
- **Black-Box Nature:** It can be difficult to interpret the decision-making process of neural networks.
- **Overfitting:** Neural networks can be prone to overfitting, especially with limited data.

Neural networks have revolutionized the field of machine learning, enabling breakthroughs in various domains. By understanding the underlying principles and leveraging their power, we can build intelligent systems capable of solving complex problems.

FIVE

THE MACHINE LEARNING PIPELINE

SIX

THE FUTURE OF MACHINE LEARNING

Deep Learning:

Deep Learning is a subset of machine learning that utilizes artificial neural networks with multiple layers to learn complex patterns from data. These deep neural networks have the ability to learn hierarchical representations, enabling them to tackle intricate tasks that traditional machine learning algorithms struggle with.

Key Concepts in Deep Learning:

- **Deep Neural Networks:** Neural networks with multiple hidden layers.
- **Activation Functions:** Non-linear functions that introduce non-linearity into the network, allowing it to learn complex patterns. Examples include ReLU, sigmoid, and tanh.
- **Backpropagation:** An algorithm used to optimize the weights and biases of the neural network by minimizing the error between the predicted output and the actual output.
- **Gradient Descent:** An optimization algorithm used to update the weights and biases during training.

Types of Deep Learning Architectures:

1. **Convolutional Neural Networks (CNNs):**

   - Designed for image and video data.
   - Utilize convolutional layers to extract features from the input data.
   - Widely used in image classification, object detection, and image segmentation.

2. **Recurrent Neural Networks (RNNs):**

   - Designed to process sequential data, such as time series and text.
   - Use recurrent connections to capture temporal dependencies.
   - Long Short-Term Memory (LSTM) and Gated Recurrent Unit (GRU) are popular types of RNNs.

3. **Generative Adversarial Networks (GANs):**

   - Comprised of two networks: a generator and a discriminator.
   - The generator creates synthetic data, while the discriminator tries to distinguish between real and fake data.
   - Used for tasks like image generation, style transfer, and data augmentation.

4. **Transformer Networks:**

   - Utilize attention mechanisms to weigh the importance of different parts of the input sequence.
   - Have revolutionized natural language processing tasks like machine translation and text summarization.

Applications of Deep Learning:

- **Computer Vision:** Image classification, object detection, image segmentation
- **Natural Language Processing:** Text classification, sentiment analysis, machine translation
- **Speech Recognition:** Speech-to-text conversion, voice assistants
- **Healthcare:** Medical image analysis, drug discovery
- **Autonomous Vehicles:** Self-driving cars
- **Financial Services:** Fraud detection, algorithmic trading

Deep learning has significantly advanced the field of artificial intelligence, enabling machines to perform tasks that were once thought to be the exclusive domain of humans. As the field continues to evolve, we can expect even more groundbreaking applications in the future.

Generative AI:

Generative AI is a subset of artificial intelligence that focuses on creating new content, such as text, images, music, and video. It leverages advanced machine learning models to generate human-quality content.

Key Techniques in Generative AI:

1. **Generative Adversarial Networks (GANs):**

   - Comprising a generator and a discriminator, GANs learn to generate realistic data.
   - The generator creates new data, while the discriminator evaluates its authenticity.
   - Applications: Image generation, style transfer, video synthesis.

2. **Variational Autoencoders (VAEs):**

   - Learn a latent representation of data.
   - Can generate new data points by sampling from the latent space.

- ○ Applications: Data generation, anomaly detection.

3. **Large Language Models (LLMs):**

   - ○ Trained on massive amounts of text data.
   - ○ Can generate human-quality text, translate languages, write different kinds of creative content, and answer your questions in an informative way.

4. **Diffusion Models:**

   - ○ A relatively new technique that involves adding noise to data and then gradually denoising it to generate new data.
   - ○ Capable of generating high-quality images and text.

Applications of Generative AI:

- **Content Creation:** Generating articles, poems, scripts, and code.
- **Design:** Designing logos, graphics, and architectural designs.
- **Media and Entertainment:** Creating realistic images, videos, and music.
- **Healthcare:** Generating synthetic medical data for training models.
- **Education:** Creating personalized learning materials.

Challenges and Ethical Considerations:

- **Misinformation and Disinformation:** The potential for generating misleading or harmful content.
- **Copyright and Intellectual Property:** Issues related to the ownership of generated content.
- **Bias and Fairness:** Ensuring that generated content is unbiased and fair.

As generative AI continues to evolve, it has the potential to revolutionize various industries. However, it's important to address the ethical implications and ensure responsible use of this powerful technology.

Ethical Implications of AI:

As AI systems become increasingly sophisticated and integrated into various aspects of our lives, ethical considerations have become paramount. Some of the key ethical concerns include:

Bias and Fairness

- **Algorithmic Bias:** AI systems can perpetuate biases present in the data they are trained on. This can lead to discriminatory outcomes, especially in areas like hiring, lending, and criminal justice.
- **Fairness Metrics:** Developing and implementing metrics to measure fairness and mitigate bias is crucial.
- **Data Diversity:** Ensuring that training data is diverse and representative can help reduce bias.

Transparency and Explainability

- **Black-Box Models:** Many AI models, particularly deep neural networks, are complex and difficult to interpret.
- **Explainable AI:** Developing techniques to understand the decision-making process of AI models can help build trust and accountability.
- **Model Interpretability:** Using techniques like feature importance analysis and visualization can help explain the model's predictions.

Privacy and Security

- **Data Privacy:** Protecting sensitive data used to train and operate AI systems is essential.

- **Data Security:** Ensuring the security of AI systems and preventing unauthorized access to data.
- **Surveillance and Privacy:** Balancing the benefits of AI-powered surveillance with potential privacy concerns.

Job Displacement and Economic Impact

- **Automation:** AI-powered automation can lead to job displacement in certain industries.
- **Skill Gap:** The increasing reliance on AI necessitates new skills and training.
- **Economic Inequality:** The benefits of AI may not be distributed evenly, leading to increased economic inequality.

Addressing Ethical Concerns

To address these ethical challenges, it is crucial to:

- **Develop Ethical Guidelines:** Establish clear ethical guidelines for AI development and deployment.
- **Promote Transparency and Accountability:** Make AI systems more transparent and accountable for their decisions.
- **Foster Collaboration:** Encourage collaboration between AI researchers, policymakers, and ethicists.
- **Educate the Public:** Raise awareness about AI's potential benefits and risks.
- **Invest in Research:** Continue to invest in research to develop more ethical and responsible AI systems.

By proactively addressing these ethical issues, we can harness the power of AI for the betterment of society while mitigating potential negative consequences.

The Role of Humans:

The rise of artificial intelligence (AI) has sparked discussions about the future of work and the role of humans in a technology-driven world. While AI has the potential to automate many tasks, it's important to recognize that humans and machines are best suited to work together, complementing each other's strengths.

Humans as the Architects of AI

Humans play a crucial role in:

- **Data Collection and Curation:** Gathering and preparing high-quality data is essential for training AI models.
- **Algorithm Development:** Designing and refining algorithms to improve AI performance.
- **Model Training and Optimization:** Fine-tuning models to achieve desired outcomes.
- **Ethical Considerations:** Ensuring that AI systems are developed and used ethically.
- **Interpretation and Decision-Making:** Understanding the insights generated by AI and making informed decisions.

The Human-Machine Partnership

Human-machine collaboration can lead to significant benefits:

- **Enhanced Productivity:** AI can automate routine tasks, freeing up human workers to focus on more creative and strategic work.
- **Improved Decision-Making:** AI can provide valuable insights and predictions, helping humans make more informed decisions.
- **Increased Innovation:** By combining human creativity with AI's computational power, new innovations can be accelerated.
- **Enhanced Problem-Solving:** AI can assist in identifying patterns and trends that humans may miss.

The Future of Work

As AI continues to evolve, the nature of work will change. Humans will need to develop new skills, such as critical thinking, creativity, and emotional intelligence, to thrive in this new era.

Here are some potential roles for humans in the age of AI:

- **AI Trainers and Developers:** Building and maintaining AI systems.
- **AI Ethicists:** Ensuring AI is developed and used responsibly.
- **AI Explainers:** Interpreting the results of AI models and communicating them to non-technical audiences.
- **AI Strategists:** Identifying opportunities to leverage AI for business advantage.
- **Creative Problem-Solvers:** Using AI as a tool to generate new ideas and solve complex problems.

By embracing collaboration between humans and machines, we can unlock the full potential of AI and create a future where technology serves humanity.

SEVEN

RECAP OF KEY CONCEPTS

A Recap of Key Machine Learning Concepts
Fundamental Concepts

- **Machine Learning:** A field of artificial intelligence that empowers systems to learn from data and make decisions or predictions without explicit programming.
- **Supervised Learning:** Learning from labeled data to make predictions or classifications.
- **Unsupervised Learning:** Discovering hidden patterns in unlabeled data.
- **Reinforcement Learning:** Learning through trial and error, interacting with an environment to maximize rewards.

Key Algorithms and Techniques

- **Linear Regression:** Predicting numerical values.
- **Logistic Regression:** Classifying data into categories.
- **Decision Trees:** Making decisions based on a tree-like structure.
- **Random Forest:** Combining multiple decision trees for improved accuracy.

- **Support Vector Machines (SVM):** Finding optimal decision boundaries.
- **Naive Bayes:** Classifying based on probability theory.
- **K-Nearest Neighbors (KNN):** Classifying based on similarity.
- **Neural Networks:** Mimicking the human brain.
- **Deep Learning:** A subset of machine learning that uses deep neural networks for complex tasks.
- **Generative AI:** Creating new content like text, images, and music.

Important Considerations

- **Data Quality and Quantity:** High-quality data is essential for training effective models.
- **Feature Engineering:** Creating informative features can significantly improve model performance.
- **Model Selection:** Choosing the right algorithm for the task at hand.
- **Hyperparameter Tuning:** Optimizing model performance by tuning hyperparameters.
- **Model Evaluation:** Assessing model performance using appropriate metrics.
- **Model Deployment:** Integrating models into real-world applications.
- **Ethical Considerations:** Addressing bias, fairness, and transparency in AI.
- **Human-Machine Collaboration:** Leveraging the strengths of both humans and machines.

By understanding these fundamental concepts and techniques, you can effectively apply machine learning to solve a wide range of real-world problems.

The Journey Continues:

The world of machine learning is vast and ever-evolving. As you've delved into the fundamentals, it's time to embark on a deeper exploration. Here are some avenues to consider:

Deepen Your Understanding

- **Dive into specialized techniques:** Explore advanced topics like transfer learning, attention mechanisms, and reinforcement learning.
- **Master popular frameworks:** Gain hands-on experience with TensorFlow, PyTorch, and other frameworks to build complex models.
- **Experiment with different algorithms:** Try different algorithms and techniques to find the best solution for your specific problem.
- **Participate in online communities:** Engage with other machine learning enthusiasts on forums, social media, and online communities.

Practical Applications

- **Build real-world projects:** Apply your knowledge to practical projects, such as image classification, natural language processing, or recommendation systems.
- **Participate in competitions:** Compete in machine learning competitions like Kaggle to test your skills and learn from others.
- **Contribute to open-source projects:** Contribute to open-source machine learning projects to collaborate with other developers and learn from their code.

Ethical Considerations

Bias and Fairness:

Bias and fairness are crucial considerations in AI. Biased data and algorithms can lead to discriminatory outcomes. To ensure fairness:

- **Diverse and Representative Data:** Use diverse datasets to avoid biases.
- **Fair Algorithms:** Design algorithms that minimize bias and promote fairness.
- **Regular Evaluation:** Continuously monitor models for bias and take corrective actions.
- **Ethical Considerations:** Prioritize ethical principles in AI development and deployment.

Privacy and Security: Privacy and security are paramount in AI. Protect sensitive data by:

- **Data Minimization:** Collect and store only necessary data.
- **Strong Security Measures:** Implement robust security protocols to safeguard data.
- **Privacy-Preserving Techniques:** Use techniques like differential privacy and encryption.
- **Transparent Practices:** Be transparent about data usage and privacy policies.

Transparency and Explainability:
Transparency and explainability are essential for building trust in AI.

- **Interpretable Models:** Use simple models or techniques like feature importance analysis.
- **Explainable AI (XAI):** Employ XAI techniques to understand model decisions.
- **Visualizations:** Use visualizations to communicate model insights effectively.
- **Documentation:** Document the model development process and decision-making.

Remember, the key to mastering machine learning is continuous learning and experimentation. By exploring these areas further, you can stay ahead of the curve and make significant contributions to the field.

The Potential of Machine Learning to Shape the Future

Machine Learning (ML) is revolutionizing industries and shaping the future in profound ways. Here are some key areas where ML is poised to make a significant impact:

Healthcare

- **Personalized Medicine:** Tailoring treatments based on individual genetic makeup and medical history.
- **Disease Diagnosis:** Early detection of diseases like cancer through image analysis.
- **Drug Discovery:** Accelerating the drug discovery process by identifying potential drug candidates.

Finance

- **Fraud Detection:** Identifying fraudulent transactions in real-time.
- **Algorithmic Trading:** Automating trading decisions based on market trends and patterns.
- **Risk Assessment:** Assessing creditworthiness and investment risks.

Transportation

- **Autonomous Vehicles:** Developing self-driving cars and trucks.
- **Traffic Optimization:** Improving traffic flow and reducing congestion.
- **Logistics and Supply Chain:** Optimizing supply chain operations and delivery routes.

Education

- **Personalized Learning:** Tailoring educational content to individual student needs.
- **Intelligent Tutoring Systems:** Providing personalized tutoring and feedback.
- **Automated Grading:** Automating the grading of assignments and exams.

Environmental Science

- **Climate Modeling:** Predicting climate change and its impacts.
- **Natural Disaster Prediction:** Early warning systems for natural disasters like hurricanes and earthquakes.
- **Environmental Monitoring:** Monitoring environmental factors like air and water quality.

Entertainment

- **Content Recommendation:** Suggesting personalized content based on user preferences.
- **Content Creation:** Generating creative content, such as music, art, and literature.
- **Virtual and Augmented Reality:** Enhancing immersive experiences.

As ML continues to advance, we can expect to see even more innovative applications that will transform the way we live and work. However, it's important to address ethical considerations, such as bias, fairness, and privacy, to ensure that ML is used responsibly and for the benefit of society.

EIGHT
CONCLUSION

In this introduction to machine learning, we've explored the fundamental concepts, algorithms, and applications that power this transformative technology. From simple linear regression to complex deep neural networks, machine learning has the potential to revolutionize industries and solve complex problems. As we've seen, machine learning is not just about technical prowess; it's also about ethical considerations and responsible development. It's crucial to use AI for the betterment of society, ensuring fairness, transparency, and accountability. The future of machine learning is bright, and its impact on our lives is only just beginning. By understanding the basics and staying curious, you can be part of this exciting journey. So, let's continue to explore the possibilities and shape the future together.

NINE

REFERENCES

1. Badillo, S., Banfai, B., Birzele, F., Davydov, I. I., Hutchinson, L., Kam-Thong, T., ... & Zhang, J. D. (2020). An introduction to machine learning. Clinical pharmacology & therapeutics, *107*(4), 871-885.
2. Alpaydin, E. (2020). Introduction to machine learning. MIT press.
3. Murphy, K. P. (2022). Probabilistic machine learning: an introduction. MIT press.
4. Alpaydin, E. (2021). Machine learning. MIT press.
5. Choi, R. Y., Coyner, A. S., Kalpathy-Cramer, J., Chiang, M. F., & Campbell, J. P. (2020). Introduction to machine learning, neural networks, and deep learning. Translational vision science & technology, *9*(2), 14-14.
6. Greener, J. G., Kandathil, S. M., Moffat, L., & Jones, D. T. (2022). A guide to machine learning for biologists. Nature reviews Molecular cell biology, *23*(1), 40-55.
7. Barto, A. G. (2021). Reinforcement Learning: An Introduction. By Richard's Sutton. SIAM Rev, 6(2), 423.
8. Zhou, Z. H. (2021). Machine learning. Springer nature.
9. Bell, J. (2020). Machine learning: hands-on for developers and technical professionals. John Wiley & Sons.
10. Lauriola, I., Lavelli, A., & Aiolli, F. (2022). An introduction to deep learning in natural language processing: Models, techniques,

and tools. Neurocomputing, 470, 443-456.

11. Sarker, I. H. (2021). Machine learning: Algorithms, real-world applications and research directions. SN computer science, 2(3), 160.

12. Sharma, N., Sharma, R., & Jindal, N. (2021). Machine learning and deep learning applications-a vision. Global Transitions Proceedings, 2(1), 24-28.

13. Ernst, D., & Louette, A. (2024). Introduction to reinforcement learning. Feuerriegel, S., Hartmann, J., Janiesch, C., and Zschech, P, 111-126.

14. Kreuzberger, D., Kühl, N., & Hirschl, S. (2023). Machine learning operations (mlops): Overview, definition, and architecture. IEEE access, 11, 31866-31879.

15. Jiang, T., Gradus, J. L., & Rosellini, A. J. (2020). Supervised machine learning: a brief primer. Behavior therapy, 51(5), 675-687.

16. MacEachern, S. J., & Forkert, N. D. (2021). Machine learning for precision medicine. Genome, 64(4), 416-425.

17. Maulud, D., & Abdulazeez, A. M. (2020). A review on linear regression comprehensive in machine learning. Journal of Applied Science and Technology Trends, 1(2), 140-147.

18. Janiesch, C., Zschech, P., & Heinrich, K. (2021). Machine learning and deep learning. Electronic Markets, 31(3), 685-695.

19. Emmanuel, T., Maupong, T., Mpoeleng, D., Semong, T., Mphago, B., & Tabona, O. (2021). A survey on missing data in machine learning. Journal of Big data, 8, 1-37.

20. Arp, D., Quiring, E., Pendlebury, F., Warnecke, A., Pierazzi, F., Wressnegger, C., ... & Rieck, K. (2022). Dos and don'ts of machine learning in computer security. In 31st USENIX Security Symposium (USENIX Security 22) (pp. 3971-3988).

www.ingramcontent.com/pod-product-compliance
Lightning Source LLC
Chambersburg PA
CBHW020442160726
48196CB00081B/42